Who Was
Woodrow Wilson?

Who Was Woodrow Wilson?

By Margaret Frith

Illustrated by Andrew Thomson

Grosset & Dunlap
An Imprint of Penguin Random House

To Norman, my brave Bermudian brother—MF

To Rhia—AT

We gratefully acknowledge Christopher Duncan's suggestion for this title—The Editors

GROSSET & DUNLAP
Penguin Young Readers Group
An Imprint of Penguin Random House LLC

Text copyright © 2015 by Margaret Frith. Illustrations copyright © 2015 by Penguin Random House LLC. All rights reserved. Published by Grosset & Dunlap, an imprint of Penguin Random House LLC, 345 Hudson Street, New York, New York 10014. GROSSET & DUNLAP is a trademark of Penguin Random House LLC. Printed in the USA.

Library of Congress Cataloging-in-Publication Data is available.

ISBN 978-0-448-48428-0   10 9 8 7 6 5 4 3 2 1

Contents

Who Was
Woodrow Wilson?

When Woodrow Wilson was almost four years old, he was playing outside his home in Augusta, Georgia. A man rushed by. He was shouting the news that Abraham Lincoln had been elected president, and war was coming.

The little boy ran inside to ask his father what it all meant. His father explained that Northern states were going to fight against Southern states. (Wilson would later say that this was his earliest memory as a child.)

Sure enough, a few months later, the bitter Civil War broke out in 1861. It lasted four years.

More than fifty years later, Woodrow Wilson became president of the United States. He was facing another horrible war. In 1914, World War I broke out in Europe. Germany was fighting Great Britain, France, Italy, Russia, and other countries, some as far away as Japan.

For three years, Wilson kept the United States out of the war. But more and more passenger ships carrying Americans across the Atlantic were being torpedoed by German submarines. In 1917, the United States joined the war. Victory came sooner with America in the fight.

In 1918, President Wilson went to Europe for the Paris Peace Conference. The nations that had won the war were planning for Germany and the rest of Europe's future. Wilson had an idea for what he called the League of Nations. He hoped the League would prevent more wars.

According to him, countries needed to work together to keep peace. It was a wonderful idea. Sadly for Wilson, the US Congress stopped the country from joining. It was a terrible disappointment for the president. Still, in 1920, President Woodrow Wilson was awarded the Nobel Peace Prize. Many consider him to be one of America's greatest presidents.

Chapter 1
A Southern Boyhood

Thomas Woodrow Wilson was born on December 28, 1856, late at night in Staunton, Virginia. His mother wrote to her father that Tommy was "a fine healthy boy . . . and as fat as he can be. Everyone tells us he is a *beautiful* boy."

Tommy had two older sisters, Marion and Annie. His father, Joseph, was a minister. His mother, Jessie, came from a family of ministers as well.

The Wilsons had been in Staunton for about a year when the family was invited to visit Georgia. While there, Dr. Wilson gave a sermon at a church in Augusta. He was a tall, handsome, outgoing man

with a strong voice. The church liked him so much, he was invited to become their minister. Dr. Wilson accepted and the family moved south.

When the Civil War started in 1861, Union forces from the North fought against Confederate soldiers of the South. Augusta was not attacked, but wounded Southern soldiers were brought there. So were Northern prisoners of war on their way to the terrible prison at Andersonville, Georgia. Dr. Wilson set up a hospital for the wounded in the church.

Schools in Augusta were closed because of the war, so Tommy's father taught him at home. Dr. Wilson often took Tommy on visits to factories and businesses around the city.

His father asked him questions about what he had seen. Wilson said that his father was the "best teacher I ever had."

As for his mother, Tommy was her favorite child. "My mother was a mother to me in the fullest, sweetest sense of the word." His older sisters were never jealous of their brother. Like their mother, they adored him. So did his younger brother, Joseph, who was born when Tommy was eleven.

Mrs. Wilson worried about Tommy. He had stomach problems and bad colds. He also suffered from bad headaches, just as she did.

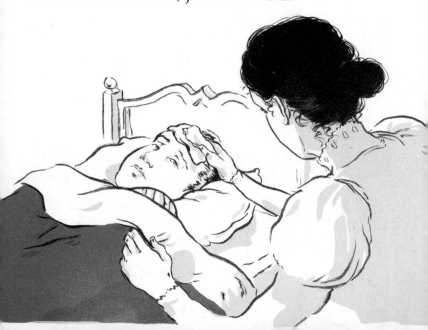

CIVIL WAR COMES TO AUGUSTA

ONE OF THE MAIN REASONS FOR THE CIVIL WAR WAS SLAVERY. MANY PEOPLE IN THE SOUTH OWNED SLAVES TO WORK ON PLANTATIONS. ABRAHAM LINCOLN WAS AGAINST SLAVERY. ONCE HE BECAME PRESIDENT, SOUTHERN STATES BROKE AWAY FROM THE COUNTRY. ELEVEN STATES FORMED THEIR OWN COUNTRY— THE CONFEDERATE STATES OF AMERICA. THE SOUTH LOST

ABRAHAM LINCOLN

THE WAR IN 1865 AND THE UNITED STATES BECAME ONE COUNTRY AGAIN. EIGHT-YEAR-OLD TOMMY WILSON WATCHED AS NORTHERN GUARDS WALKED JEFFERSON DAVIS THROUGH THE SILENT STREETS OF AUGUSTA. DAVIS HAD BEEN PRESIDENT OF THE CONFEDERACY, BUT NOW HE WAS A PRISONER.

Tommy's mother could see that he was a slow learner. He didn't know the letters of the alphabet until he was nine. He couldn't read on his own until he was eleven.

Right after the war ended, a school for boys opened in a warehouse near the Wilsons. Tommy went, but he wasn't that interested in lessons. He liked playing outdoors with his friends a lot more.

Baseball was new to Augusta. All the boys
wanted to be on a team. Tommy was small, yet he
was good enough to play second base. He started
a club with his friends. He liked taking over and
being the leader.

The boys called their club the "Light Foot Base Ball Club." They met up in a hayloft. Tommy wrote a "constitution" with rules. If the boys didn't follow them, there were fines to pay. If a boy swore, he had to put five cents in a jar. If he missed a meeting, he owed ten cents.

Tommy liked to have others obey his rules. That didn't mean he always behaved himself or did what he was supposed to. One day Tommy heard that the circus was in town.

He and his friends skipped school. They spent the day following the elephant parading around the city. Before going back to school, they padded the seats of their pants with cotton. Back then, teachers were allowed to spank children. The padding would make the spanking hurt less. Tommy didn't mind being punished. It was one of his best days ever.

Chapter 2
Off to College

Tommy was fourteen when Dr. Wilson was offered a job as a professor in Columbia, South Carolina. He would teach young men to become preachers.

The Wilsons lived in Columbia for less than four years. At sixteen, Tommy began to enjoy learning. New ideas set his imagination racing.

Tommy was still a slow reader,

but it didn't stop him from reading as much as he could. Handwriting didn't come easy, either. He practiced and practiced. He wrote his name again and again until he liked the way it looked. Then he found out about shorthand. Shorthand symbols made it easier to write faster. Tommy no longer got behind taking notes in class.

The Wilsons left Columbia and moved to Wilmington, a seaport in North Carolina. Soon Tommy was off to Davidson College, also in North Carolina.

Tommy turned seventeen in 1874. He had never lived on his own before. He kept track of every penny he spent along with lists—of his clothes, his class schedule, books he borrowed, and letters he wrote.

In the spring, Tommy went home with a fierce cold. He was also still battling headaches. He felt too sick to go back to Davidson. Instead he stayed at home and studied.

Tommy and his father spent happy hours together. During one of their long talks, Tommy told his father that he had made a wonderful discovery. He had discovered that he had "a mind, sir. I've found I have an intellect and a first class mind."

Tommy started thinking about returning to college. James McCosh was a family friend who was president of the College of New Jersey in a small town called Princeton. Once during a visit to the Wilsons, Dr. McCosh had told Tommy's father, "The boy'll be comin' to Princeton, no doubt."

Dr. McCosh turned out to be right. Tommy was eighteen when he arrived at Princeton.

JAMES McCOSH

Chapter 3
Heading North

Princeton was almost as old as Harvard and Yale, two of America's finest universities. It was an all-male school. Many of the boys were from rich families. They were confident and outgoing. Having a good time was more interesting to them than getting good grades. Tommy stayed in the background, watching and listening.

PRINCETON UNIVERSITY

Tommy went to his first class expecting a lively discussion. To his surprise, he found that the professor just presented facts that the students were expected to memorize. The professors didn't encourage students to think on their own. Tommy was bored. Still, he paid attention and earned good grades.

What did excite Tommy was history and politics. Once he read a book about the history of England. It talked about Samuel Pepys in the seventeenth century. Pepys wrote a famous journal that covered ten years of important events such as the Great Fire of London and the Great Plague of London.

SAMUEL PEPYS

It inspired Tommy to start his own journal in shorthand.

At Princeton, Tommy joined a debating society called the American Whig Society. A debate is an "argument" with rules. The debaters take opposite sides on a subject. A judge decides who wins the argument. Tommy chose Whig over other debate teams because it concentrated on politics. He would become one of Whig's strongest debaters. An old friend described "the fire in his eyes" when Tommy stepped up to argue a point of view.

Tommy had never seen a football game before going to Princeton. The very first game he went to made him a fan. He went to all the games and cheered loudly. Still, baseball remained his favorite sport.

The campus newspaper, *The Princetonian*, also became an important part of Tommy's student life. He began writing columns for the paper. In his third year, he took over as managing editor. The staff quickly saw that he liked to make decisions. "He was boss and deserved to be," one of them said.

Tommy studied hard and stayed in the top third of his class. He had a 90.3 average and graduated with honors. He would go on to law school, but always in the back of his mind he dreamed of a career in politics. Not only was he interested in what was happening in the county, he wanted to take part in changing the country, making it a better place.

Chapter 4
Down South Again

UNIVERSITY OF VIRGINIA

In the fall of 1879, Tommy entered the School of Law at the University of Virginia in Charlottesville. He was not eager to become a lawyer, but he had to earn a living.

At twenty-two, Tommy decided he wanted to be called by his middle name—Woodrow.

Woodrow hadn't been around girls much during his years at Princeton. He longed for a girlfriend. He wrote to a friend that he was "still a poor lone laddie with no fair lassie."

Woodrow spent his free time with his cousins nearby in Staunton, Virginia. It didn't take long for him to fall in love with Hattie Woodrow.

She was smart and lively, and they enjoyed each other's company. But when he confessed his love for her, she was surprised. She thought of him as a friend. Woodrow was brokenhearted.

Once again Woodrow suffered from stomachaches and colds that wouldn't go away. In his second year, he went home to Wilmington for Christmas feeling terrible. His mother and father persuaded him not to go back to Charlottesville.

After a year and a half of studying on his own, Woodrow was ready to practice law. He decided go to Atlanta, Georgia, a growing southern city.

Woodrow didn't like practicing law any better than he had studying it. He began thinking about becoming a college professor. He wanted to teach history and political science—the study of how governments work. He applied to graduate school at Johns Hopkins University in Baltimore, Maryland, and was accepted.

JOHNS HOPKINS
UNIVERSITY

Before he left Atlanta, he went to Rome, Georgia, for his mother. Her brother had died. She asked Woodrow to take care of his affairs. One Sunday morning in Rome, Woodrow went to church. Across the aisle, he saw a young woman with "a bright pretty face." He was struck with her "splendid, mischievous, laughing eyes."

It turned out that her father was the minister. Woodrow had planned to introduce himself to Reverend Axson after the service. Now he could hardly wait to meet his daughter, Ellen Louise.

Woodrow spent as much time as he could with Ellen. Not only was she pretty, she was smart, a talented artist, and had read even more books than he had. She was just the kind of girl he wanted to marry.

Once home in Wilmington, Woodrow found reasons to go to Georgia as often possible. One day after a picnic in a meadow outside of Rome,

Woodrow told Ellen, "You were the only woman I had ever met to whom I felt that I could open all my thoughts." He was falling in love.

Woodrow asked Ellen to marry him and she accepted. They both knew they would have to wait. Woodrow had two years of graduate school ahead of him.

Woodrow pushed himself hard at Johns Hopkins. His parents worried that he would get sick if he didn't slow down. Not only was he studying to be a professor, he was also working on a book about the branches of government.

BRYN MAWR COLLEGE

At last, Woodrow was ready to look for a job. He wrote to Princeton, but they didn't need any new teachers. A college for women was opening in Pennsylvania. It was called Bryn Mawr. He was offered a position at a good salary.

At last, Woodrow and Ellen could start a life together. On June 24, 1885, they were married in Ellen's grandparents' house in Savannah, Georgia.

Chapter 5
Back Up to Princeton

The Wilsons arrived at Bryn Mawr in September 1885. Right away Woodrow was popular with his students and the other teachers. A young woman later said that Wilson was "the most interesting and inspiring college lecturer I have ever heard." Students looked forward to his warm smiles and jokes.

In April 1886, Ellen went home to Georgia
to give birth to Margaret. The following year in
August, the Wilsons' second daughter, Jessie, was
born.

These happy times, however, were clouded by
the death of Woodrow's mother on April 15, 1888.

She had never healed properly from a bad fall in 1886. Still her death was unexpected and very hard on Woodrow.

After the Wilsons had been at Bryn Mawr for three years, Wesleyan University in Middletown, Connecticut, asked Woodrow to join their faculty. Woodrow accepted.

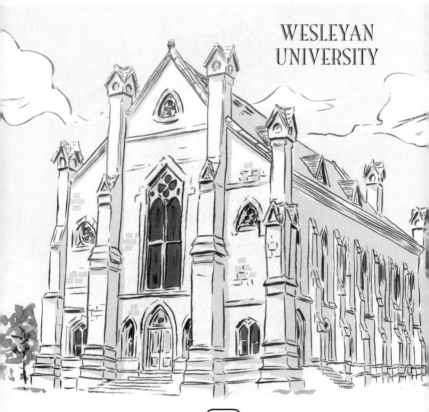

WESLEYAN
UNIVERSITY

During the Wilsons' stay in Middletown, their third daughter was born. They named her Eleanor, but they called her "Nell."

Woodrow didn't stay at Wesleyan long, because Princeton came calling. In the fall of 1890, he arrived back on the campus excited and ready to teach.

Teaching there had not changed much since Woodrow's student days. That didn't stop Woodrow from coming up with fresh ideas for his own classes on law and politics. Young men who tried to test the new teacher by acting up in class were soon won over. More and more students wanted to hear Woodrow's lectures. "At the close of a lecture, they would often cheer him," one boy said.

Woodrow and his family were happy at
Princeton. He was as much in love with Ellen
as ever. Nell remembered wonderful days with
everyone together: "Father had a certain
spontaneous gaiety, a delicious sense of fun and
mischief."

In May 1896, a sharp pain raced down Woodrow's right arm to his hand. His fingers became numb. He was worried. He saw a doctor who advised him to give his hand a long rest.

Ellen was worried, too. Was Woodrow working too hard? How could she get him to slow down? She thought a trip away from the bustle of Princeton would be the best medicine. Woodrow's doctor agreed. Soon it would be summer. Ellen persuaded him to go by ship to Scotland. She would stay home and take care of the girls. He would be away for three months.

Sailing across the Atlantic took a restful twelve days. By the end of the crossing, Woodrow's hand was no longer bothering him.

He visited Carlisle in England, where his mother was born. He rode a bicycle to the Lake District in the north and fell in love with this beautiful area. It had the highest mountain in England and the longest, deepest lakes. He wrote many love letters to his Ellen.

Woodrow returned in early September in time to get ready for the 150th anniversary of Princeton University. President Grover Cleveland would be there along with famous professors from all over America. Some were coming from as far away as Europe.

Woodrow gave a speech at the opening day celebration. He called it "Princeton in the Nation's Service." How proud Ellen was when he spoke. "It was the most brilliant, dazzling, success from first to last. And such an ovation as Woodrow received!" she wrote to her cousin Mary.

Perhaps Woodrow was even more excited
that afternoon when the Princeton football team
defeated the University of Virginia, 48–0.

At the closing of the three-day celebration, the president of the college—Patton—announced that the name of the College of New Jersey would be changed. The college was now officially Princeton University.

Chapter 6
University President

More and more, Wilson was invited to lecture at universities around the country. He was a compelling speaker full of ideas and much in demand.

At Princeton, President Patton made no effort to improve education. When asked why, Patton blamed it on a lazy attitude among the students. "Gentlemen, whether we like it or not, we shall have to recognize that Princeton is a rich man's college and that rich men frequently do not come to college to study."

The Board of Trustees was losing patience with Patton. They thought *he* had a lazy attitude. In 1902, they agreed that it was time for him to resign.

Woodrow Wilson was nominated to take Patton's place. The entire board voted for him. At age forty-five, he became the thirteenth president of Princeton.

A celebration for the new president took place on October 25, 1902. Important Americans from all walks of life, a proud Princeton faculty, and an enthusiastic student body were there. (Because of a carriage accident, President Theodore Roosevelt was not able to attend.)

When Wilson was introduced, everyone stood and clapped for nearly ten minutes.

President Wilson spoke about what Princeton and other universities could contribute to the nation. In offering a top-rate education, he said, "We are planning for the country." He knew that as the nation grew, it needed intelligent, educated citizens. "Universities of the country must take part in supplying them," he told the crowd.

Woodrow's eighty-year-old father was in poor health and living with the Wilsons. Sadly, that very night Dr. Wilson suffered severe chest pains. For the next three months, he stayed in bed. Almost every night, Woodrow sat beside his father, singing his favorite hymns. Dr. Wilson died on January 21, 1903.

Wilson's father was who had fired up Woodrow's mind as a young boy. That was what Wilson now wanted to do for his college students. In a speech to New York graduates, called alumni, he said that he wished "to transform thoughtless boys performing tasks into thinking men."

In a bold move, Wilson added fifty talented young tutors to the faculty. For the different courses, professors gave lectures two days a week. Now, on the other days, students met with their tutors for lively discussions in small groups.

Wilson worked harder than ever teaching, giving speeches, writing books, and raising money from alumni around the country. One new professor said, "What had been called a high-class country club began to be a real university."

In 1910, after a long battle, Wilson lost the support of the board and the alumni on where to put a new graduate school. It was the second time the board had not supported a proposal he cared deeply about, a change involving the Eating Clubs.

Wilson was discouraged. Maybe it was time for a change. In a letter to Ellen, he wrote wistfully: "It would be rather jolly, after all, to start out in life anew together, to make a new career, would it not?"

EATING CLUBS

EATING CLUBS AT PRINCETON BEGAN IN 1879. STUDENTS FROM WEALTHY FAMILIES WERE INVITED TO JOIN THESE FANCY CLUBS WITH NAMES LIKE "IVY" AND "CAP AND GOWN." PRESIDENT WILSON SAID THE CLUBS ENCOURAGED MEMBERS TO IGNORE THE OTHER STUDENTS. HE WANTED YOUNG MEN FROM ALL BACKGROUNDS TO MIX WITH ONE ANOTHER. HE PROPOSED REPLACING THE PRIVATE CLUBS WITH EATING HALLS ON CAMPUS. HE DIDN'T SUCCEED. THERE ARE STILL EATING CLUBS AT PRINCETON TODAY.

Chapter 7
A Path to the Presidency

In the spring of 1910, an opportunity came along that made Wilson think seriously about switching careers. The Democrats of New Jersey were in search of a candidate for governor. The past five governors of the state had all been Republicans. It was time for a new face. They talked to Wilson. Would he consider running?

Wilson was fascinated by politics, but he wasn't yet a politician himself. New Jersey politics were rough. The most powerful Democrat in the state was "Sugar Jim" Smith Jr.

"SUGAR JIM" SMITH J[

He was the boss. He ran a party machine—an organization that did crooked business with the state government and big companies in New Jersey. But Wilson had done a lot to make Princeton a source of great pride for the state.

Although he had never run for any office, now was his chance to work for changes in government. On his own, Wilson began giving passionate speeches to groups of bankers, Democratic Party supporters, and to Progressives—Democrats who wanted to make the New Jersey state government more honest.

During the summer, Wilson talked over the idea with his family and close friends at Princeton. All agreed he should run for governor. In the end, Wilson said that he would not put his name forward. But if the Democrats chose him, he would agree to be their candidate and run in the election.

The candidate would be chosen at the

Democratic convention in the state capital of Trenton. On September 15, Sugar Jim's machine got behind Wilson. He won easily.

The Progressives at the convention were disappointed in Wilson. They had hoped for someone who could fight the party bosses. Now they were certain that Wilson was under the thumb of the party machine.

When Wilson walked up to the podium to speak, the Progressives slumped in their seats. Sugar Jim and his men looked up from the front row with smug smiles on their faces. They expected Wilson to do whatever they wanted.

But when Wilson spoke, he surprised both wings of the party—the machine politicians and the Progressives. "We are witnessing . . . a revival of the power of the people," he said. Many in the audience jumped to their feet and cheered. Now the Progressives were smiling. Maybe—at last—here was someone who would represent the voters, not the bosses.

When Sugar Jim and his men tried to tell Wilson what issue to talk about, Woodrow Wilson listened politely. He didn't argue, but he went his own way and campaigned for what he believed in.

On November 8, polling places were filled with people anxious to vote. By ten o'clock in the evening, Wilson got the news that he had defeated Republican Vivian M. Lewis. Lewis was the State Banking and Insurance Commissioner. It was a landslide victory. Fifteen of the twenty-one New Jersey counties went for Wilson.

The new governor wasted no time living up to his promises. He got to know the men in the New Jersey legislature. Like the US Congress, the legislature had two houses. Laws had to pass both houses.

Wilson knew he was facing a state senate that had more Republicans than Democrats. It would not be easy to get them to vote his way, but he was persuasive. Within three months, new laws were passed.

A law called the Geran bill made elections fairer. Now there were secret ballots. People felt freer to vote for whomever they wanted. Anyone hoping to be a candidate had to win a primary election in their party before the general election. This meant that voters—not party bosses—chose candidates.

The legislature passed Wilson's corrupt-practices bill. Candidates could only spend a certain amount of money on their campaigns. They had to tell how much money they had. Big business could not give money to political campaigns.

A workers-compensation bill meant that workers who were injured on the job had to be paid.

Because of Wilson, political machines lost power in New Jersey. He worked hard each day and looked forward to relaxing at home in the evenings. He read to the family, as his father had during Woodrow's childhood. Sometimes the family sang around the piano together. Wilson loved music and had a beautiful voice. But when he recited silly limericks one right after another, Margaret, Jessie, and Nell couldn't stop laughing.

Wilson had not been governor for long when politicians and ordinary citizens began to talk about him running for president. They saw what he was doing for New Jersey. He would be a good president for the country, they said.

William Howard Taft, a Republican, was the current president. The next election was only two years away, in 1912.

Three powerful Princeton friends approached Wilson. Could they raise

WILLIAM HOWARD TAFT

money for him and convince people to vote for him for president? *Yes*, he said. He also traveled to other cities to meet and shake hands with voters.

They were attracted to this charming man who cared for the people.

It was time for the Democratic Convention in Baltimore, Maryland, in June 1912. Wilson competed for the nomination against men whose names were better known than his. Even so, his ideas for reforming government were popular.

On July 2, Wilson became the Democratic candidate for president.

The fight for the White House began. It was an unusual race. Besides Governor Wilson for the Democrats and President Taft for the Republican Party, there were two other candidates. Theodore Roosevelt had been president from 1901 to 1909. A former Republican and friend of Taft's, he wanted to be president again. He was running for what was called the Bull Moose Party. And there was also Eugene Debs, who had run twice before and represented workers and their unions.

THEODORE ROOSEVELT

Wilson campaigned on his New Freedom platform that promised everyone in the country an equal chance at getting ahead. It was a hard-fought race, but Wilson emerged the winner on November 5. Roosevelt came in second, Taft third, and Debs a distant fourth.

Wilson would not be sworn in as president until March 4, 1913. He had four months to prepare. He wanted to think about who might run the departments in his cabinet.

In a wise move, Wilson took his family on a month's vacation to Bermuda, a British island in the Atlantic Ocean. It was not Wilson's first trip to the island. He had made friends there, writer Mark Twain among them.

The Wilsons rented a house that looked out over a clear turquoise sea. Ellen painted. Woodrow played golf or rode his bicycle along the narrow, winding roads with Jessie and Nell.

They sailed back, arriving in New Jersey on December 16. Wilson was about to become one of the most powerful men on earth. In less than ten years, Woodrow Wilson had gone from president of Princeton University, to governor of New Jersey, to president of the United States. He was fifty-five years old.

Chapter 8
Living in the White House

It was gray and overcast when Taft and Wilson rode down Pennsylvania Avenue in Washington, DC, in a horse-drawn carriage. Excited crowds cheered and waved.

In front of the Capitol building, Wilson was sworn in as the twenty-eighth president of the United States. His hand rested on Ellen's bible. The new president looked out at a crowd of one hundred thousand people. "There has been a change of government," he began.

In a strong voice Wilson told the audience about his ideas for making government better. He closed on a serious note instead of victorious one. "This is not a day of triumph," he said. "It is a day of dedication."

The rest of the day and evening was filled

with much handshaking and congratulations. After midnight, a servant found the new president standing in his bedroom at the White House. He was in his underwear looking around with a puzzled expression. Where were his pajamas?

They were in a trunk left behind at the railroad station. When the pajamas finally arrived, a sound-asleep president, still in his underwear, did not wake up to put them on.

Wilson had been in office only five days when he came down with a severe headache and stomach pains. The White House doctor was called. His name was Cary Grayson. Right away he took Wilson off his medicines, including a new drug called aspirin.

DR. CARY GRAYSON

When Wilson was well enough to return to work, Dr. Grayson came up with a plan for staying healthy—rest as much as possible, eat foods that didn't upset his stomach, get a good night's sleep, take relaxing rides in the car, play golf.

Wilson tried to do as Dr. Grayson said. Relaxing and getting plenty of sleep, however, weren't easy for someone who was the president of the United States.

Playing golf was something he did as often as he could. He liked to play with Dr. Grayson and they became friends for life. (During the winter, the Secret Service painted golf balls black so the president could practice in the snow.)

Wilson was anxious to get to work on his New Freedom platform.

He started with tariffs. These were taxes on goods that came into the United States from other countries. Wilson wanted lower tariffs to make goods cheaper.

Wilson proposed a new banking system. The Federal Reserve Act was responsible for making it easier to borrow money and preventing banks from going out of business.

An antitrust act called for a commission that would make businesses, big and small, act fairly.

Wilson brought back the practice of speaking to Congress in person about the state of the country. Since the early 1800s, presidents had written out a State of the Union speech. It was sent to Congress and read out loud by a clerk. Wilson thought he should speak for his own ideas, and that has remained the custom since Woodrow Wilson.

Also for the first time, reporters were invited to ask questions at a press conference. It was held at the White House in the Oval Office where the president worked. One hundred twenty-five reporters showed up. They found the president relaxed and welcoming. He answered most of their questions. Between March and December 1913, he held sixty press conferences.

SIGN HERE, PLEASE

ON OCTOBER 3, 1913, FIFTY GUESTS IN EVENING CLOTHES WAITED FOR THE PRESIDENT IN THE OVAL OFFICE. EVERYONE CLAPPED WHEN HE WALKED IN AND SAT DOWN AT HIS DESK. HE LOOKED WITH PLEASURE AT THE TARIFF BILL PRINTED ON PARCHMENT WAITING FOR HIS SIGNATURE.

TWO GOLD PENS LAY NEXT TO THE BILL. HE USED ONE TO SIGN HIS FIRST NAME, THE OTHER FOR HIS LAST NAME. THEN HE GAVE THE PENS TO TWO CONGRESSMEN WHO HAD WORKED HARD TO GET THE BILL PASSED. SIGNING BILLS WITH DIFFERENT PENS IS A TRADITION THAT PRESIDENTS CARRY ON TO THIS DAY.

As for Mrs. Wilson, it was not in her nature to be outgoing and social. She wanted to be a different kind of First Lady. There were things she wanted to do beyond hosting parties.

How did poor people live in city slums, crowded and hidden from the wealthy areas of the city? She wanted to help. She began by urging Congress to pass a bill to clear out the slums.

One morning, the First Lady and her daughters were admiring the formal gardens from her bedroom window. Suddenly Mrs. Wilson got an idea. She would plant a rose garden. Her husband would pass by it whenever he walked along the covered walkway to his office. The Rose Garden has become a beloved spot at the White House.

In December 1913, Dr. Grayson thought that Woodrow and Ellen both looked tired.

He persuaded them to go south for Christmas. They did so. Yet when they came home, Ellen was still weak and tired.

All through the spring, Woodrow was "dreadfully worried" about Ellen. When she didn't get any better, Dr. Grayson called in other doctors. Ellen had a serious kidney disease. There was nothing they could do.

Ellen slowly got worse. On Thursday, August 6, she seemed to know that the end was near. She kept asking Woodrow about her slum-clearance bill. He asked Congress to pass it that day, which they did.

When Woodrow told Ellen, she smiled. She died around five o'clock in the afternoon.

Ellen had been married for twenty-nine years to the man she once told her brother was "the greatest man in the world." Ellen was fifty-four.

Woodrow was brokenhearted. How could he go on without her?

Chapter 9
"He Kept Us Out of War"

Wilson was lonely and depressed. He missed his darling Ellen. It was hard to concentrate on the country's business, but he had to now more than ever.

In late July 1914, Germany had declared war on France, Russia, and Great Britain. Neither Wilson nor the American people wanted the United States to join the war in Europe. Wilson was determined to keep the country neutral. That meant that it would not take sides.

In 1915, the *Lusitania,* a British passenger ship, was struck by two German torpedoes off the southern coast of Ireland. One hundred twenty-eight Americans were on board and lost their lives.

The submarine attacks didn't stop. More Americans lost their lives. They were not soldiers, just ordinary citizens. People in the United States were in an uproar. Wilson feared the country might have to join the war. The pressure on him was building.

When he could get away from his busy office, Wilson liked to take drives around Washington. One afternoon Wilson was out for a drive with

Dr. Grayson. A woman waved at the doctor as the car drove by. Woodrow asked who the beautiful woman was. Her name was Edith Galt. She was a widow, sixteen years younger than Woodrow.

Soon after, Dr. Grayson quietly arranged an "accidental" meeting. He and the president went off to play golf. When they returned, Edith was at the White House having tea with one of Woodrow's cousins.

Edith and Woodrow began seeing each other. The more time they spent together, the more Woodrow enjoyed being with Edith. When he finally asked her to marry him, she said yes. They were married in a small ceremony at Edith's home with their families looking on. That night they traveled by train to Hot Springs, Virginia, for their honeymoon.

The next morning, the president's Secret Service agent saw Woodrow in his tailcoat and

EDITH GALT

top hat, dancing a little jig. Suddenly he clicked his heels in the air and started singing a hit song of the day: "Oh, you beautiful doll! You great big, beautiful doll!" The agent turned around and quietly hurried away.

In 1916, Wilson won a second term as president. He made the phrase "He kept us out of war" the motto of his campaign.

Across the ocean, the Battle of Verdun was raging in France. It was the bloodiest battle of the war. It went on for ten months. Over eight hundred thousand French and German soldiers were killed or wounded.

In January 1917, Wilson was shown a secret telegram that British spies had gotten hold of. It revealed that Germany was trying to persuade Mexico to side with them in the war. In return, Germany would help Mexico take back territory lost to the United States in 1848. Wilson was outraged.

A month later Germany ordered submarines to sink as many ships as possible. It didn't matter if the ships were American. The Germans were taking a chance that the United States would stay neutral no matter what. But they were wrong.

During March, seven American merchant ships were torpedoed. Wilson knew the time had come for the country to go to war.

He went to Congress. "The world must be made safe for democracy," Wilson said. Congress agreed. On April 6, the United States declared war on Germany.

Chapter 10
Preparing for War

Was the United States ready for war? No. Wilson saw that a much larger army was needed. Over 100 million people lived in the United States with a small army of 190,000.

Men were called up to become soldiers, or "doughboys," a nickname from the Mexican-American War. It would take time to build a large, well-trained army.

Wilson asked farmers to grow all the food they could.

Not only did they have to feed the people at home, but food needed to be sent overseas for the soldiers. Food in America was rationed. This meant that people could only buy a certain amount. To have enough food, families grew victory gardens.

With so many soldiers in Europe, women took jobs that men had done. They worked in businesses like banks or phone companies, and in factories like steel mills and ammunition factories. Some worked as airplane mechanics.

The government sold Liberty Bonds to raise money for the war.

Woodrow gave Edith a small flock of sheep. The sheep kept the grass on the White House lawn trimmed, and "White House wool" was auctioned off. It raised almost $100,000, which the Wilsons gave to the Red Cross.

On January 8, 1918, Wilson presented his Fourteen Points to Congress. They were goals for when the war was over. One was for a League of Nations. Wilson's hope was that countries would join the League and work for world peace.

By August 1918, a million and a half US soldiers had landed in France. The Allies were exhausted from four years of brutal war in the trenches. They welcomed the doughboys, who helped defeat the Germans. By the end of the war in November, over two million American soldiers had joined the war.

The Battle of the Argonne Forest in France would be the last battle. It began on September 26 and went on for forty-seven hard-fought days. The fighting stopped on November 11, 1918.

In the five months the United States fought, over 116,516 Americans were killed and 204,002 were wounded.

The final end to the war wouldn't come until

terms for peace were settled and a treaty signed. On December 4, the president and the first lady sailed across the Atlantic to attend the Paris Peace Conference. In France, excited crowds welcomed the president as their hero.

Woodrow and Edith visited Italy and Great Britain. Everywhere they went, grateful crowds were waiting for Wilson.

When the Paris Peace Conference began in January 1918, two thousand people lined up in the rain to see the American president walk through the grand entrance of the Ministry of Foreign Affairs.

THE FIGHTING DOUGHBOYS

NO ONE IS SURE WHERE SOLDIERS GOT THE NAME *DOUGHBOYS*. IT VERY LIKELY CAME FROM THE FOOT SOLDIERS MARCHING ACROSS THE DESERT IN NORTHERN MEXICO DURING THE MEXICAN-AMERICAN WAR. AS THEY WALKED ALONG, FINE WHITE SAND SWIRLED AROUND THEM. THEY LOOKED AS IF THEY WERE COVERED IN FLOUR FROM HEAD TO TOE. THE NICKNAME *DOUGHBOYS* STUCK.

WOODROW WILSON

GEORGES CLEMENCEAU

DAVID LLOYD GEORGE

VITTORIO ORLANDO

The "Big Four" dominated the meetings—
Georges Clemenceau of France, David Lloyd
George of Great Britain, Vittorio Orlando of Italy,
and Woodrow Wilson.

Settling territories was at the top of the list. War had changed the borders of countries. It was a difficult business, deciding on new borders and settling disagreements over which country would get what pieces of land.

Wilson concentrated on getting support for the League of Nations. What finally brought the council around was one important point. Member nations would provide security for one another. If a country was attacked, the other countries would come to its defense.

Discussion about the terms of the treaty went on and on. The Big Four kept changing their minds about how Germany should be punished for the war. Wilson was exhausted from all the arguing.

He came down with a fever, severe headaches, coughing, and stomach pains. Did he have the flu? His mind was hazy and confused. Was he having small strokes in his brain?

Fortunately, Wilson got better. After six long months, the treaty was ready. On June 28, 1919, the Wilsons drove outside Paris to Versailles where a gigantic palace had been built in the late 1600s. The signing took place in the magnificent Hall of Mirrors.

The next day, Woodrow and Edith boarded a ship called the *George Washington*. Wilson was sure that his dream of a League of Nations was a step closer to becoming true.

VERSAILLES

Chapter 11
Fighting for the League

At home, Woodrow Wilson faced a big problem. The Treaty of Versailles was in danger. It needed to be passed by the Senate. Many of the senators were against it because of the League of Nations. "Dare we reject it and break the heart of the world?" Wilson asked when he addressed the Senate.

Why were the senators against the League of Nations? Mostly because of the rule that member nations had to protect one another. Why should the United States have to provide security for countries on the other side of the Atlantic?

Henry Cabot Lodge,

HENRY CABOT LODGE

a powerful Republican senator, disliked Wilson and his policies. He saw to it that change after change was made to the treaty.

Wilson's answer was to travel ten thousand miles by train to twenty-nine cities in western states. He would talk directly to the American people. Those close to him, especially Dr. Grayson, were against the trip. Wilson needed to rest. Not even Edith could make the president stay home.

Crowds of Americans, both Democrats and Republicans, flocked to hear Wilson. He could feel the tide turning in support of the League.

But as the days went by, Dr. Grayson and Edith realized the president was very ill. He admitted that his left arm and leg felt numb. The tour was cut short, and a disappointed Wilson returned to the White House.

On October 2, his fourth day at home, Edith noticed that Woodrow's left hand had gone limp.

WOMEN AND THE VOTE

IN 1920, THE NUMBER OF PEOPLE IN THE UNITED STATES WHO COULD VOTE DOUBLED. THAT WAS BECAUSE OF AN AMENDMENT—OR CHANGE—TO THE CONSTITUTION GRANTING WOMEN THE RIGHT TO VOTE. AT FIRST, WOODROW WILSON HAD NOT BEEN A STRONG SUPPORTER OF THE CAUSE. HIS ATTITUDE CHANGED AFTER WOMEN BEGAN PROTESTS IN FRONT OF THE WHITE HOUSE. IN 1918, WILSON SPOKE TO CONGRESS IN FAVOR OF WOMEN VOTING. STILL, IT TOOK TWO YEARS BEFORE THE NINETEENTH AMENDMENT WAS PASSED.

She went to phone Dr. Grayson. When she came back, Woodrow was passed out on the floor.

A stroke had partly paralyzed the left side of his body. Only the doctors, family, and close advisers knew how serious Wilson's condition was. The country was told that the president was exhausted. Nothing more.

A difficult decision had to be made. If a

president can't carry out his duties, the vice president takes over. Although Wilson couldn't leave his bed, his mind was clear.

The doctors said that Wilson could work while he was getting better. This was a relief to Vice President Thomas Marshall. The last thing he wanted was the responsibility of being president.

Edith understood the president's work and what he thought about issues. For the previous four years, she had gone over important papers with him in the mornings. After dinner, they worked together again.

Only Dr. Grayson and Wilson's chief of staff knew that Edith was showing the president what he needed to see, sign, or make a decision about. Sometimes she even made decisions by herself. She wanted her husband to get well. She would do whatever she could to help him.

After a month, Wilson was sitting up in a chair in his bedroom. He began to see a few members of his cabinet.

The Senate went on debating the Treaty of Versailles. The treaty was voted down in March 1920. The vote was forty-nine to thirty-five. The president was devastated. In November, there would be another election. Should he run for the third time? In his heart, Woodrow Wilson knew it was not possible.

On Inauguration Day in March 1921, Wilson rode in a car from the White House to the Capitol with the next president, Republican Warren Harding. Because Woodrow couldn't climb the stairs to the swearing in, Edith and Woodrow didn't stay for the ceremonies.

That afternoon, over five hundred people gathered in front of their new home on S Street to cheer Wilson. Friends from the government stopped in to wish him well.

The next day thousands more came. As the crowds waved, he smiled and waved back with a white handkerchief.

The Wilsons lived a quiet life in their new house. Woodrow bought a black car from the White House fleet for afternoon drives. He had his initials painted over the presidential seal on the doors. The eagle on the hood was replaced with a tiger. A tiger is Princeton's mascot.

Music and reading filled Woodrow and Edith's evenings. They spent three peaceful years together.

In early January 1924, Edith knew that Woodrow's health was failing and called Dr. Grayson. But it was no use. Wilson grew sicker, and on February 3, he died at home. He was sixty-seven years old. He was buried in the Washington National Cathedral.

In 1956, the dean of the cathedral, the Very Reverend Francis B. Sayre Jr., presided over a special ceremony. Wilson's casket was moved to another place in the cathedral. Reverend Sayre was Woodrow Wilson's grandson.

REVEREND FRANCIS B. SAYRE JR.

In 1923, Francis Sayre, then eight, was out driving with his grandfather when someone called out, "I'm for the League!" Francis shouted back in an excited voice, "I'm for the League!"

"Grandfather didn't say a word," he remembered. "He just dissolved into tears for reasons I didn't understand, pulled me into his arm, and kissed me on the forehead."

THE BIRTH OF THE UNITED NATIONS

IN THE 1920S AND 1930S, STRONG COUNTRIES BEGAN PULLING OUT OF THE LEAGUE OF NATIONS. BY 1939, IT HAD NO POWER TO PREVENT THE SECOND WORLD WAR. IN EARLY 1942, THE UNITED STATES, GREAT BRITAIN, THE SOVIET UNION (RUSSIA), AND CHINA ALONG WITH TWENTY-TWO OTHER NATIONS SIGNED A UNITED NATIONS AGREEMENT. (PRESIDENT FRANKLIN ROOSEVELT COINED THE TERM "UNITED NATIONS.") THEY PROMISED TO FIGHT GERMANY AND OTHER ENEMY

NATIONS. THE WAR ENDED IN 1945. THE UNITED NATIONS OFFICIALLY CAME INTO BEING ON OCTOBER 24 WITH FIFTY-ONE MEMBERS. TODAY THERE ARE 192 MEMBERS.

TIMELINE OF
WOODROW WILSON'S LIFE

1856 — Woodrow Wilson is born in Staunton, Virginia, on December 28

1859 — Moves to Augusta, Georgia

1875 — Enters the College of New Jersey, now called Princeton University

1881 — Moves to Atlanta, Georgia, to practice law

1883 — Enters Johns Hopkins University in Baltimore, Maryland

1885 — Marries Ellen Louise Axson

1886 — First child Margaret is born, followed by Jessie in 1887, Eleanor in 1889

1890 — Joins the faculty at Princeton

1902 — Becomes president of Princeton University

1910 — Becomes governor of New Jersey

1913 — Becomes president of the United States

1914 — Wife Ellen dies of Bright's disease

1915 — Marries Edith Bolling Galt

1917 — Reelected president for a second term

1918 — Reads his Fourteen Points in a speech to Congress in January

1919 — Attends the Paris Peace Conference
Collapses in the White House from a paralyzing stroke

1920 — Awarded the Nobel Peace Prize

1921 — The Wilsons move to a house on S Street

1924 — Dies on February 3

TIMELINE OF THE WORLD

Abraham Lincoln becomes president — **1860**

The American Civil War begins — **1861**

The Civil War ends and Abraham Lincoln dies on April 15 — **1865**

Alfred Nobel invents dynamite — **1866**

The Suez Canal links the Mediterranean with the Red Sea — **1869**

Thomas Alva Edison invents the incandescent lightbulb — **1879**

Mark Twain's *The Adventures of Huckleberry Finn* is published — **1884**

A fifteen-year-old Irish immigrant is the first passenger to pass through Ellis Island — **1892**

The founder of the Red Cross, Henry Dunant, and French economist Frederic Passy are awarded the first Nobel Peace Prize — **1901**

The Wright brothers make their first flight at Kitty Hawk — **1903**

The Great San Francisco Earthquake — **1906**

The *Titanic* sinks on April 15 — **1912**

World War I begins in Europe — **1914**

The Treaty of Versailles ends World War I — **1919**

The Nineteenth Amendment to the US Constitution gives women the right to vote — **1920**

The United Nations begins on October 24 — **1945**

The League of Nations is dissolved — **1946**

BIBLIOGRAPHY

Berg, A. Scott. **Wilson**. New York: G. P. Putnam's Sons, 2013.

Cooper, John Milton, Jr. **Woodrow Wilson: A Biography**. New York: Knopf, 2009.

MacMillan, Margaret. **Paris 1919: Six Months That Changed the World**. New York: Random House, 2002.

Smith, Gene. **When the Cheering Stopped: The Last Years of Woodrow Wilson**. Alexandria, VA: Morrow, 1964.